3 1994 01470 2341

2/12

SANTA ANA PUBLIC LIBRARY

D0575791

LIFE STORIES / BIOGRAFÍAS

ROSA PARKS

Gillian Gosman

Traducción al español: Eduardo Alamán

PowerKiDS
press

New York

Published in 2011 by The Rosen Publishing Group, Inc.
29 East 21st Street, New York, NY 10010

Copyright © 2011 by The Rosen Publishing Group, Inc.

All rights reserved. No part of this book may be reproduced in any form without permission in writing from the publisher, except by a reviewer.

First Edition

Editor: Jennifer Way
Book Design: Ashley Burrell and Erica Clendening

Spanish translation: Eduardo Alamán

Photo Credits: Cover (inset) William Philpott/Getty Images; cover (background), pp. 6–7, 12–13, 14–15, 17, 22 (left) Don Cravens/Time & Life Pictures/Getty Images; pp. 4–5 Paul Schutzer/Time & Life Pictures/Getty Images; p. 8 Russell Lee/MPI/Getty Images; pp. 8–9 Hulton Archive/Getty Images; p. 10 FPG/Hulton Archive/Getty Images; pp. 10–11 Anthony Potter Collection/Getty Images; pp. 13, 16–17, 22 (right) Grey Villet/Time & Life Pictures/Getty Images; pp. 18–19 Rolls Press/Popperfoto/Getty Images; pp. 20–21 Jeff Kowalsky/AFP/Getty Images.

Library of Congress Cataloging-in-Publication Data
Gosman, Gillian.
 [Rosa Parks. Spanish & English]
 Rosa Parks / by Gillian Gosman. — 1st ed.
    p. cm. — (Life stories = Biografías)
 Includes index.
 ISBN 978-1-4488-3218-7 (library binding)
 1. Parks, Rosa, 1913-2005—Juvenile literature. 2. African American women—Alabama—Montgomery—Biography—Juvenile literature. 3. African Americans—Alabama—Montgomery—Biography—Juvenile literature. 4. Civil rights workers—Alabama—Montgomery—Biography—Juvenile literature. 5. Montgomery (Ala.)—Biography—Juvenile literature. 6. Montgomery Bus Boycott, Montgomery, Ala., 1955-1956—Juvenile literature. 7. African Americans—Civil rights—Alabama—Montgomery—History—20th century—Juvenile literature. 8. Segregation in transportation—Alabama—Montgomery—History—20th century—Juvenile literature. 9. Montgomery (Ala.)—Race relations—Juvenile literature. I. Title.
 F334.M753P373613 2011
 323.092—dc22
 [B]

                                    2010035358

Web Sites: Due to the changing nature of Internet links, PowerKids Press has developed an online list of Web sites related to the subject of this book. This site is updated regularly. Please use this link to access the list:
www.powerkidslinks.com/life/rparks/
Manufactured in the United States of America
CPSIA Compliance Information: Batch #WW11PK: For Further Information contact Rosen Publishing, New York, New York at 1-800-237-9932

Contents

Contenido

MEET ROSA PARKS

Rosa Parks is often called the mother of the **civil rights movement**. How did one person come to stand for this important cause?

Parks was brave and hardworking. She believed in the **equality** of all people and all races. She put her life on the line to fight for her beliefs.

Rosa Parks worked with many civil rights leaders, such as Martin Luther King Jr.

Rosa Parks es conocida como la madre del **movimiento de los derechos civiles**. ¿Sabes cómo una persona pudo convertirse en representante de una causa tan importante?

Parks fue valiente y muy trabajadora. Parks creía en la **igualdad** de todas las personas y todas las razas. Parks puso su vida en peligro para luchar por sus creencias.

Rosa Parks trabajó con muchos líderes de los derechos civiles, como Martin Luther King Jr.

Young Rosa

Rosa Louise McCauley was born on February 4, 1913, in Tuskegee, Alabama. When she was two, the family moved to Pine Level, Alabama.

Rosa left high school when her grandmother and mother fell ill. She went back to high school and finished when she was 21. In 1932, she married a barber named Raymond Parks and took his name, becoming Rosa Parks.

Parks worked as a seamstress for many years. A seamstress is a person who sews clothing.

Rosa Louise McCauley nació el 4 de febrero de 1913, en Tuskegee, Alabama. Cuando ella tenía dos años, la familia se mudó a Pine Level, Alabama.

Rosa dejó la escuela secundaria cuando su abuela y su madre se enfermaron. Rosa volvió a la escuela y terminó a los 21 años. En 1932, Rosa se casó con un barbero llamado Raymond Parks. Rosa tomó el apellido de su esposo, convirtiéndose en Rosa Parks.

Parks trabajó como costurera durante muchos años. Una costurera es una persona que cose prendas de vestir.

Life in a Segregated America

Rosa Parks lived during the time of **segregation**. Whites and blacks went to different schools. They even had to sit in different parts of buses. There was fear and hate between the races. Sometimes there was **violence**.

Parks and many others wanted to end segregation. The actions that these **activists** took were called the civil rights movement. They used nonviolent **resistance**, including **sit-ins** and **boycotts**.

Water fountains were segregated during this time. The things for African Americans were often marked "colored."

En aquel tiempo las fuentes de agua eran segregadas. A menudo, las cosas que eran para los afroamericanos se marcaban con letreros que decían "de color".

This man is standing in front of a store at which only white people were allowed to shop.

Este hombre está de pie en el frente de una tienda en la que sólo se le permitía entrar a ciudadanos blancos.

VIDA DURANTE LA SEGREGACIÓN

Parks vivió durante la época de la **segregación**. En aquella época los blancos y los negros iban a escuelas diferentes, e incluso tenían que sentarse en diferentes zonas en los autobuses. En aquella época, había miedo y odio entre las razas. A veces había **violencia**.

Parks y otros querían acabar con la segregación. Las acciones que estos **activistas** tomaron para combatir la segregación se conocen como el movimiento de los derechos civiles. Estos activistas usaron una **resistencia** pacífica con **boicots** y **sentadas**.

The Parkses' Politics

Raymond and Rosa Parks spoke out against unfair treatment and gave their time to different causes. They studied nonviolent resistance. They took part in workshops, or classes, on how to have a peaceful **protest**.

Raymond and Rosa were members of the National Association for the Advancement of Colored People, or the NAACP. Rosa was the secretary and youth leader for the Montgomery chapter.

These NAACP members are protesting a club that refused to serve African Americans.

Estos miembros de la NAACP protestan afuera de un club que se negaba a servir a los afroamericanos.

The NAACP has chapters all over the United States. This is an NAACP office from the late 1940s.

La NAACP tiene capítulos en todo el país. Ésta es una oficina de la NAACP a finales de los años 1940.

Las ideas de la familia Parks

Raymond y Rosa Parks se manifestaron en contra del trato injusto. Juntos estudiaron la resistencia pacífica y tomaron clases sobre cómo **protestar** de manera pacífica.

Raymond y Rosa eran miembros de la Asociación Nacional para el Avance de la Gente de Color, o NAACP, por su sigla en inglés. Rosa fue la secretaria y líder de la juventud en el capítulo de la ciudad de Montgomery.

Planning a Protest

The civil rights activists of Montgomery wanted to lead a boycott of the city's segregated bus lines. The boycott would cause the city to lose money. If the city lost enough money, it might change its unfair law.

Civil rights leaders wanted someone to be the face of the boycott. They wanted someone serious and smart, like Rosa Parks.

Here is Parks (center) at a meeting led by Martin Luther King Jr. (left).

Aquí vemos a Parks (centro) en una reunión con Martin Luther King Jr. (izquierda).

Many people who took part in the bus boycott walked instead of taking the bus.

Muchas personas que participaban en el boicot a los autobuses caminaron en lugar de tomar el autobús.

Planeando una protesta

Los activistas de los derechos civiles de Montgomery querían hacer un boicot de las líneas de autobuses segregados de la ciudad.

El boicot haría que la ciudad perdiera dinero. Si la ciudad perdía suficiente dinero podría cambiar la legislación. Los líderes querían a alguien que fuera la cara del boicot. Estos líderes buscaban a alguien confiable e inteligente, como Rosa Parks.

Breaking the Law!

On December 1, 1955, Rosa Parks boarded a Montgomery bus. She had just finished a long day of work. On her bus ride home, Parks refused to give her seat to a white rider.

The bus driver ordered the black riders to give up their seats to make room for more white riders. Parks refused. She was **arrested** for breaking Alabama's segregation law.

This picture shows Parks (far right) riding a Montgomery bus after the boycott ended.

¡Contra la ley!

El primero de diciembre de 1955, Rosa Parks se subió a un autobús de Montgomery. Parks acababa de terminar un largo día de trabajo. En el autobús, Parks se negó a darle su asiento a un pasajero blanco.

El conductor del autobús ordenó a los pasajeros negros que cedieran sus asientos a los pasajeros blancos. Parks se negó a ceder su asiento y fue **arrestada** por infringir la ley de segregación de Alabama.

Esta foto muestra a Parks (extrema derecha) en un autobús de Montgomery al finalizar el boicot.

The Montgomery Bus Boycott

After her arrest, Rosa Parks was taken to the police station and charged with breaking Alabama's segregation law. That night, civil rights activists, led by Martin Luther King Jr., met to plan the bus boycott.

The bus boycott began four days later. Boycotters walked and carpooled instead of taking the bus. After 381 days, a court decided that Montgomery's segregated buses were illegal.

Montgomery's buses were nearly empty during the boycott.

Durante el boicot, los autobuses de Montgomery estaban casi vacios.

The Montgomery bus boycott lasted 381 days. During that time, many boycotters walked to work, even when it rained.

El boicot de autobuses de Montgomery duró 381 días. En ese tiempo, muchas personas que apoyaban el boicot caminaron a su trabajo, incluso bajo la lluvia.

EL BOICOT DE MONTGOMERY

Tras su arresto, Parks fue trasladada a la comisaría de policía donde se le acusó de quebrantar la ley de segregación en Alabama. Esa noche, los activistas de derechos civiles, liderados por Martin Luther King Jr., se reunieron para planificar el boicot a los autobuses.

El boicot comenzó cuatro días más tarde. Sus participantes caminaron y compartieron sus autos en lugar de tomar el autobús. Después de 381 días, un tribunal decidió que los autobuses segregados de Montgomery eran ilegales.

A Great First Step

The Montgomery bus boycott was an important moment in the civil rights movement. Rosa Parks helped get it started.

During the boycott, civil rights activists were treated with fear and hate. In the end, the boycott showed whites that the activists were serious. It showed the activists that if they worked together, they could change unfair laws.

The 1960s brought new civil rights laws. Here President Lyndon B. Johnson (seated) signs the Civil Rights Act of 1968 into law.

Un gran paso

El boicot a los autobuses fue un momento importante en el movimiento de los derechos civiles. Rosa Parks ayudó a ponerlo en marcha.

Durante el boicot, los activistas de los derechos civiles fueron tratados con miedo y odio. Al final, el boicot demostró que los activistas actuaban en serio. Los activistas demostraron que trabajando juntos podían cambiar leyes injustas.

La década de 1960 trajo nuevas leyes de derechos civiles. Aquí el presidente Lyndon B. Johnson (sentado) firma en ley el Acta de Derechos Civiles de 1968.

Life After the Boycott

After the boycott, the Parks family moved to Detroit, Michigan. Rosa got a job in the office of African-American congressman John Conyers Jr. She worked for him from 1965 until 1988.

In the 1980s, Parks created a number of groups and **scholarships** for young people. She wrote the story of her life. She gave many public speeches, too. Rosa Parks died on October 24, 2005. She was 92 years old.

Parks was given a Congressional Gold Medal in 1999 to honor her work for civil rights.

Tras el boicot, la familia Parks se mudó a Detroit, Michigan. Rosa consiguió un trabajo en la oficina del congresista afroamericano John Conyers Jr. Parks trabajó para Conyers Jr. de 1965 a 1988.

En la década de 1980, Parks creó una serie de grupos y **becas** para beneficio de la juventud. Parks escribió la historia de su vida y dio muchos discursos públicos. Rosa Parks falleció el 24 de octubre de 2005. Parks tenía 92 años.

Parks recibió la Medalla de Oro del Congreso en 1999, como reconocimiento a su trabajo por los derechos civiles.

Timeline / Cronología

February 4, 1913
4 de febrero de 1913

Rosa Louise McCauley is born in Tuskegee, Alabama.

Rosa Louise McCauley nace en Tuskegee, Alabama.

December 1, 1955
1 de diciembre de 1955

Parks refuses to give up her bus seat and is arrested.

Parks se niega a dar su asiento en el autobús y es arrestada.

December 5, 1955
5 de diciembre de 1955

The Montgomery bus boycott begins.

Comienza el boicot de los autobuses de Montgomery.

October 24, 2005
24 de octubre de 2005

Rosa Parks dies.

Muere Rosa Parks.

1965

Parks begins working in Congressman John Conyers's office in Detroit.

Parks comienza a trabajar con el congresista John Conyers en Detroit.

December 20, 1956
2 de diciembre de 1956

The Montgomery bus boycott ends.

Finaliza el boicot de los autobuses de Montgomery.

Glossary

activists (AK-tih-vists) People who take action for what they believe is right.

arrested (uh-REST-ed) Stopped a person who is thought to have committed a crime.

boycotts (BOY-kots) Refusals to deal with people, nations, or businesses.

civil rights movement (SIH-vul RYTS MOOV-mint) People and groups working together to win freedom and equality for all.

equality (ih-KWAH-luh-tee) Being equal.

protest (PROH-test) An act of disagreement.

resistance (rih-ZIS-tens) A strong stand taken against something.

scholarships (SKAH-lur-ships) Money given to people to pay for school.

segregation (seh-grih-GAY-shun) The act of keeping people of one race, sex, or social class away from others.

sit-ins (SIT-inz) Acts of protest at which generally groups of black people refuse to move out of a white-only part of a public place.

violence (VY-lens) Strong force used to hurt someone or something.

Glosario

activistas (los/las) Personas que toman acción por lo que creen que es correcto.

arresto (el) Ser privado de la libertad por quebrantar la ley.

becas (las) Dinero que se le da a una persona para que pueda asistir a la escuela.

boicots (los) Negarse a participar en alguna situación específica.

igualdad (ser) Ser igual.

movimiento de los derechos civiles (el) La iniciativa para buscar libertad e igualdad para todos.

protesta (la) Actuar ante un desacuerdo.

resistencia (la) Una fuerte posición en contra de algo o alguien.

segregación (la) El hecho de mantener a la gente de una raza, sexo o clase social, separada de los demás.

sentadas (las) Actos de protesta en los que las personas se rehusan a moverse de un lugar o espacio público.

violencia (la) Uso de la fuerza para dañar a alguien.

Index

Índice